STEPHEN CURRY

A
SHARPSHOOTER'S JOURNEY
TO THE NBA & BEYOND

WHAT IT TAKES
TO BE LIKE STEPH

An Unauthorized Biography

By Steve James

"If you don't fall how are you going to know what getting up is like."

- Stephen Curry

TABLE OF CONTENTS

INTRODUCTION

After the first three games of the 2015-2016 season Stephen Curry had scored 118 points on 68 shots. One game against the New Orleans Pelicans included scoring 53 points in 36 minutes of play. Even for the *2015 MVP and the leader of last year's championship team*, this was still a loud and impressive way to open up a season. He has opened the conversation as to who the best player is in the league, and what kind of lasting legacy he will lead.

If it were **anyone's first time watching basketball, they would be amazed.** A stunning performance is a stunning performance. But knowing Steph Curry's background and history with the sport, makes this success story all the more intriguing. Because unlike many other basketball phenoms – Michael Jordan, Lebron James, Kobe Bryant, etc. – who were scouted and sought after in their developmental years, Curry's success has come much later. And arguably, with more difficulties.

No one had heard of Curry until 2008, when sports fans were invested in one of their favorite sporting events of the year – *March Madness*. It was March 24, 2008 when 7-seed Gonzaga played Curry's team, the 10-seeded Davidson. The "baby-faced" sophomore scored 40 points, 30 of which were in the second half, and hit 8 of 10 3-pointers, to upset Gonzaga.

Davidson continued to press on. The next matchup was against the second-seeded Georgetown. Curry had a slow start to the game, scoring only 5 points in the first half, heading into the locker room losing by a substantial margin. However, he came back in the second half to score 25 and lead his team to another upset victory. The next game was against three-seeded Wisconsin. Curry put up a modest 33 points, to form a sizable lead and advance to the Elite 8. Davidson lost the next game to the Kansas Jayhawks, who would go on to win the championship that year, by two points. Curry but up a respectable 25 points, but left a mark much more extensive than a statistic. **People knew Steph Curry's name, and they wanted to know more.**

However, there are few people that would expect that Curry would become one of, and possibly the best, player in the NBA. He's a phenom not only because of his abilities, but also because of how he defied expectations regarding his size, ability, and potential. How Curry got to where he is now is not a mystery by nature. He worked hard, practiced constantly, and is now reaping the benefits in a serious way.

But what exactly did his hard work look like? What kinds of drills was he doing? How many shots a day does one of the greatest shooters of all time take? What kind of mental preparation was he enduring? These are the questions many people are left with, and what this book hopes to provide insight into. Rather than a romanticized and storied version of Curry's rise to his elite level of play, we're going to take an **in-depth view at the specific ways in which Curry has gotten to the level where he is at now**.

Further, this book seeks to inspire. Despite Steph Curry's upbringing into a sports family, with his dad as a professional basketball player, he was obviously exposed to the sport at an early age, and had certain advantages that many players don't have. That said, his rise to the top was not by any means seamless, easy, or fluid. Part of what makes Steph's story so compelling is that he has had many hiccups, and has had to overcome many obstacles along the way. By combining a mix of anecdotes about Steph's life, as well as instructional drills and diagrams, we can step into Steph's psyche and work ethic, and begin to understand both **why and how he is one of the most respected players today**.

CHAPTER 1

UPBRINGING

Born Wardell Stephen Curry II to professional basketball player Dell Curry in 1988, he has become better known as "Steph" to fans and reporters. Thus, Steph was surrounded by basketball and the culture of sports from an early age.

Dell really learned how to play basketball after his father, Steph's grandfather, made a basket of sorts with a utility pole, a fiberglass backboard, and steel brackets, outside their home in rural Virginia. The basketball hoop, which was meant to keep Dell out of trouble more than anything else, turned into an NBA career. And it was on this same hoop, that Steph too began to learn the art of shooting.

Dell moved from Fort Defiance High School in Fort Defiance, Virginia, to play for Virginia Tech. He finished his career with 2,389 points and 295 steals. Additionally, he played baseball for Virginia Tech, and was even good enough to get drafted in the 1985 MLB draft to the Baltimore Orioles. However, he turned the offer down when he was drafted 15th by the Utah Jazz in 1986.

Dell Curry guarding Michael Jordan

Dell played in the league from 1986 until 2002 for five different teams. From the Jazz he moved to the Cleveland Cavaliers, then onto Charlotte Hornets. Notably, he was the Hornet's all-time leader in points throughout his ten seasons in Charlotte. Dell then played for the Bucks for a year, and finished out his career playing for the Toronto Raptors. Thus, Curry was around a culture of basketball from a young age and took a serious interest in playing as he watched his father succeed.

Steph and Seth, who is also now a professional basketball player, used to play basketball when they went to visit their grandfather on the same rickety hoop that Dell honed his skills. Because of the conditions of the basketball hoop – a flimsy backboard, and a hard and brutal rim, hitting anything but net was a surefire way to miss a shot. Thus, **Steph learned the best way to shoot was with a high arc and good backspin.**

Further, the court on which he played was always muddy, and without any sort of wall or structure in place to block missed shots from rolling many feet away, he learned that making each shot was the key to not having to run into the woods and chase balls, as well as being the key to being able to take more shots. As he said in an in-depth ESPN magazine article about these formative years:

"It was 'make it or chase it' out there, and if you missed, it was terrible. So you didn't miss. That instills something in you as a shooter without you even knowing it's happening."

What it instilled in Steph would be something that he would carry for years to come. Patience, hard work, diligence, and unrelenting practice. These are just some of the characteristics that describe Curry.

Steph led his middle school team to an undefeated season, performing well enough for the Varsity coaches at Charlotte Christian High School to take an interest. They encouraged Steph to skip Junior Varsity and head straight for the high school team. The central theme of the doubt cast on to Steph Curry as being able to become top-tier basketball player stems from his size. **In high school, he was a mere 5'8" and weighed just 150 pounds**. He attended Charlotte Christian School, and already had dreams of playing at a high level.

A young and small Steph Curry

Though Curry could already sink more shots than most top level high school players, *his issue was his release point*. Using a flip shot, where he gained power from his belt buckle, Dell knew would be a problem, especially considering his size. This is a common issue many young players face, especially when they're small and want to shoot from the outside. **If Steph wanted any chance at getting shots off at the next level, he would need to establish a new shot.** Which, as any basketball player knows, is a decidedly difficult task that can yield a lot of frustration.

And it did for Curry. He and Dell spent one summer dedicated to changing his shot, to make him a more effective player. The key point to hammer home was that he needed to change his release point to above his head. This makes the shot significantly harder to block.

That summer was a memorable one in the Curry family, and not in a positive way. They called it *"the summer of tears"* and Steph has referred to it as **the only time in his life when he didn't like shooting.**

Dell made Steph shoot hundreds and hundreds of shots that summer, beginning his release from over his head. It was difficult, and Steph could not even shoot outside of the paint for the first three weeks. However, repetition is what Dell said would bring success. And it did. Beginning by doing basic form shooting drills near the basket where Steph would begin his release over his head, he took thousands and thousands of shots until he was able to take a few steps back and begin expanding his range. Over time, using his legs more and more, he was able to turn into a productive shooter.

However, Steph has emphasized that his father was not forceful when it came to basketball. In fact, he didn't even always want to be a basketball player. He would have to make that decision on his own, and when he did, his parents supported him. *"He wasn't ever going to push us to the gym,"* Steph says. *"Sure, he'd go with us, but it's not like he'd wake up and force us to go. That helped me a lot, because my work ethic has always been my own and not someone else forcing it on me."*

In high school, Curry led his team to three consecutive conference titles and state playoffs. He was also named All-State and All-Conference.

Curry's high school coach, Shonn Brown, said that **Steph made every practice except for one.** Brown recalls:

"He came to me and said, 'Coach, we missed one today, it was my fault, can we come early tomorrow and make it up? I said, 'Absolutely;' he and Seth came the next day at 6

a.m. and doubled their workouts ... that just showed how, off the court, he's very bright, very respectful and respected, which is proof that he was reared very well from a parenting standpoint."

Thus, even someone like Steph, who was the leader of his team and displaying a high level of skill in high school, was **the most committed player**. Few high school kids would wake up at 6 in the morning for anything, let alone to train. However, this foundational work ethic was something that Steph developed at a young age, and has carried over to his professional career.

CHAPTER 2

COLLEGE YEARS AT DAVIDSON

Despite this development, which would lead to Curry establishing the shot that has made many consider him the best shooter in the NBA, it did not put him in a position to go to a top NCAA program. **Many people, concerned about Steph's size, or lack-there-of, did not recruit him**. On his list of potential schools were William & Mary, Wofford, Winthrop, Virginia Commonwealth University, Virginia Tech, High Point, and Davidson – which he would ultimately choose.

In the last 45 years, only five NBA MVP award winners who competed at the NCAA level have come from outside the major conferences. These include players such as Steve Nash, who went to Santa Clara, Karl Malone, who went to Louisiana Tech, Willis Reed from Grambling, Julius Erving on Massachusetts, and David Robinson of Navy. These are some pretty big names. Thus, it is certainly possible to make it big after attending a school with a less-established program, but it is indeed rare. And as is always the case, other coaches are left wondering how they missed such spectacular talents.

Curry's high school coach, Shonn Brown, attributed some of this oversight to Curry's size and general stature. He said in a Yahoo news article, "*Sometimes kids don't pass the eye test. As a senior he looked like he was about 14 years old.*"

Curry had grown from 5'8", 125 pounds, to 6'1" and 160 throughout high school – a substantial margin – but not enough to get him out of the "too small" category. Even Virginia Tech, Dell's alma mater, would not offer Curry a guaranteed spot. The best they could do was offering him a chance to walk on and making him redshirt in his first year. But, for Curry, a young aspiring basketball player from North Carolina, where basketball is king, the lack of recruitment was disappointing.

One man, however, did not overlook this potential. And this was Bob McKillop, the coach of Davidson, who started looking at Curry seriously when he was in the ninth grade. McKillop showed a great interest, and promised Curry the chance to have a team built around him. And his confidence in Curry's future proved to be true. Curry signed in November 2005 and never looked back.

McKillop was interested in Curry for more than his skills. Though McKillop wrote to Curry, attempting to persuade him to come, talking about his tenacity and aggressiveness, he continued to like what he saw. At the AAU tournaments where he saw Curry, he was impressed by how much **he hustled on defense and around the court**. He would listen to his coaches intently. Instead of merely jogging over after a timeout was called, he'd sprint to the team's bench. These are attributed coaches also look for in players – things that exemplify coachability.

Further, McKillop was impressed with the values instilled in this young man that college coaches often find rare to find. When he visited the Curry home, he noticed certain character traits exemplified throughout the house. Beyond seeing that he came from a strong and supportive family, he noticed how Steph kept his room clean and in order. While this by no means directly translates to athletic success, it was a promising thing to see someone so disciplined, both on and off the court.

Steph Curry with coach Bob McKillop

However, Curry's rise to the 2008 March Madness fame did not come all at once. He started in his first collegiate game, a rare occurrence, against Eastern Michigan. Curry finished the game with 13 turnovers (and 15 points) as the Wildcats managed to eke out the win. The following evening, Curry showed his resilience, scoring 32 points, getting 9 assists, and even taking 9 rebounds, in his second collegiate game. Curry went on to average 21.5 points per game in his first season, the second freshman in the country in scoring, behind Kevin Durant.

Further, and perhaps more importantly, Curry led the Wildcats to a 29-5 record, as well as conference title. He even scored 113 three-pointers in the season, breaking the NCAA record for freshman season 3-point shots. Davidson made the tournament in his first year, but did not go very far. They grabbed a number 13 seed but lost to Maryland 82-70. Curry scored 30 points. His performances earned him awards including the ***Southern Conference Freshman of the Year, SoCon Tournament MVP,*** and ***SoCon All-tournament team.***

Steph had the fortune of growing two inches in his second year to 6'3" and continued improving. He raised his average to 25.5 points per game, and began to make his game more dynamic. With 4.7 rebounds and 2.8 assists, the Wildcats again had a successful season, finishing with a record of 26-6. Davidson entered the tournament with high hopes and a number 10 seed.

As mentioned in the introduction, Curry began gaining serious notoriety after his performance against Gonzaga. His performance was electric, scoring 40 points and going 14 of 22 from the field. Some of his shots, too, were particularly big. He hit the tie breaking 3-pointer with just a minute left in the game, as well as sinking two free throws with 14.5 seconds left to seal the deal.

Steph Curry scoring 40 points against 7-seed Gonzaga

Had Curry had a mere one-game impressive performance against Gonzaga, the media likely would not have been buzzing so much. However, this was hardly the case. The next game was against the second-seed, Georgetown. He had a rough start in the game. Newscasters were calling him tired. They said Georgetown's aggressive defense was simply too much. Curry headed to the locker room after the first half scoring only five points and missing 10 of his first 12 shots.

However, the second half was quite literally and figuratively a new ball game. Curry rallied back to score 25 points in the second half. At one point Davidson was down by 17 points, and miraculously managed to pull out a 74-70 victory. Georgetown shot 63% from the field, hardly a poor performance, but could not figure out a way to shut Curry down in the second half.

Next up on Davidson's schedule were the Wisconsin Badgers, whom the Wildcats would go on to beat handedly. It was noted that the phrase "*I can do all things*" were written on the side of Curry's sneakers at the game. Which ultimately, and clearly, rang true.

Wisconsin, a number three seed, had good credentials coming into the game. They were 31-5, and were keeping opponents to an average 53.9 points per game. Michael Flowers was cited as being a top perimeter defender, making high-scoring guards notoriously "ineffective." This, however, did not ring true.

With just under 14 minutes left to play, the game was close, 48-45. Curry made two consecutive 3-point goals, quickly giving Davidson a 9-point lead. That was Curry's 23rd point and fifth 3-pointer of the night. He did put up a few more points, ten to be precise, to finish out the game with 33 points, 3 rebounds, 4 assists, and 4 steals. Davidson won 73-56.

On March 30, it was time for Davidson to face the Kansas Jayhawks. The Jayhawks came with a plan. A four-guard rotation to prevent Curry from getting opportunities was put in place. With numerous and fresh bodies on him throughout the game, Curry had a difficult time getting good looks, but still scored 25, made 3 assists, and had 4 rebounds and a steal. Additionally, Kansas had to eke out a victory, and only won by a margin of two, the final scoring being 59-57.

Despite the fact that Kansas won the game, and would go on to win the entire tournament, the name that people had ringing in their ears was "Steph Curry." **He left his mark on the NCAA, and basketball, world in a significant way that people would not soon forget**.

Curry matching up against Kansas

With all the buzz surrounding Curry, many wondered if he would head to-wards the NBA. However, Curry opted to return for his junior year. His reason was that he wanted to improve upon certain aspects of his game. Notably, **he wanted to prove that he could be a point guard, and better his chances for a higher draft pick in the NBA.**

His decision to stay a third year at Davidson turned out to be quite produc-tive, and most argued it was a good move. He scored a career-high 44 points against Oklahoma – a game that the Wildcats lost by 4 points. He also hit the 2000-point mark in January of 2009. However, a rolled ankle in February led to a month of recovery to prepare for the post season.

The Wildcats again won the Southern Conference title but did not receive an NCAA tournament bid. They competed in the 2009 NIT tournament, but fell to Saint Mary's Gaels in the second round.

Curry finished at Davidson leaving quite a legacy. He was Davidson's all time leading scorer, with 2,488 career points. In his final season **he was the leading scorer in the NCAA with 28.6 points per game**. Additionally, he averaged 5.6 assists, and 2.5 steals.

It was after this season that he explained he would forgo his final year at Davidson in an effort to pursue his dreams of becoming a professional basketball player.

CHAPTER 3

PROFESSIONAL NBA CAREER

2009-2010

Steph Curry was selected as the **seventh overall pick in the 2009 NBA draft to the Golden State Warriors.** He would wear number 30; the same number he wore at his time at Davidson. After signing a four-year $12.7 million contract he made his debut in the NBA against the Houston Rockets on October 28, 2009. After starting and playing 36 minutes, he ended the game with 14 points, 7 assists, 4 steals, and 2 turnovers in his first professional game.

There was some turmoil as Curry joined the Warriors. Monta Ellis did not seem to welcome Steph's presence, and it was evident on the court. It took until January for Curry to really begin establishing himself as an integral part of Golden State's offense. On February 10, 2010, Curry scored 36 points, had 13 assists, and grabbed 10 rebounds, getting his first career triple-double. Another stunning performance occurred on April 7, 2010, when the coach at the time, Don Nelson, set a record for career coaching wins (1,333). The same night Curry dropped 27 points, had 14 assists, got 8 rebounds, and snagged 7 steals.

Steph Curry in his first season on the Warriors

Although Curry went on to average 17.2 points, 5.9 assists, 4.4 rebounds, and 1.9 steals for the season, his statistics after January are more indicative of the kind of player he was becoming. After January he averaged 20.6 points, 6.7 assists, and 4.8 steals per game, in his 48 starts.

Many thought he should have won the 2009-2010 NBA Rookie of the Year Award, and although he was a close contender, Tyreke Evans was decided over him. He did join the ranks of Evans and Brandon Jennings as the three unanimous picks for the All-Rookie First Team. Additionally, **Curry broke the record for 3-point goals by a rookie and shot 43% from the 3-point line.**

2010-2011 Season

Under new coach Keith Smart, the Warriors would go on to finish the 2010-2011 season with a 36-46 record, which was 3rd in the Pacific Division. Curry went on to average 18.6 points, 3.9 rebounds, 5.8 assists, and 1.5 steals per game. He scored a season high 28 points against the Minnesota Timberwolves on February 27, 2011.

A notable accomplishment came during All-Star weekend, when Steph Curry beat Derrick Rose, John Wall, and Russell Westbrook in the **Skills Challenge**.

Curry with his Skills Challenge Trophy

In addition to winning the skills challenge, Curry led the NBA in free-throw percentage, shooting 93.4%, which was also good enough to set a single-season shooting record for the Warriors, surpassing Rick Barry's prior record of 92.4%. And finally, he continued enticing people with his personal character traits, winning the **2010-2011 Sportsmanship Award**.

In short, Steph Curry was off to a bright start on his new professional career.

2011-2012 Season

However, the 2011-2012 season was not an easy one for Curry. Due to a series of ankle sprains in 2010-2011, he needed surgery to fix torn ligaments around his right foot. After rehab and training, during an exhibition game Steph reinjured himself, spraining the newly repaired ankle.

Opting to play through the pain, Curry opened the season against the Los Angeles Clippers, but it was clear he was not at the top of his game. Only scoring 4 points and going 2 for 12 from the field, was uncharacteristic of the up and coming superstar. He followed up with 21 points and 10 assists to secure a victory over the Chicago Bulls, but again hurt himself by rolling his ankle.

Curry rested 3 games before coming back to sprain his ankle again. And after another brief hiatus he came back only to strain a tendon in his foot. By March, it was clear Curry would need surgery again. It came in the form of arthroscopic surgery on his ankle, and a total of 26 of 66 games played. Although his averages – 14.7 points, 3.4 rebounds, 5.3 assists, and 1.5 steals – are nothing to be shameful of, this was certainly not the Curry that everyone knew and expected to see.

Steph Curry struggling with ankle problems in the 2011-2012 season

In order to get back healthy Curry underwent an intense rehab process with Keke Lylse, the Warrior's director of athletic performance. One key exercise that they both credit to Curry's ability to come back healthy, unexpectedly came from a yoga book. The exercise targets hip strength, which is critical in preventing lower body injuries. The exercise is *"The Single-Leg Hip Airplane"*.

Additionally, Lysle targeted Steph's core and gluteus. He suspected that Steph used his ankles to control the unpredictable and awkward movements that result when one plays basketball. One key workout that is a Lysle favorite is the trap bar deadlift, which activates the gluteus maximus.

The Single-Leg Hip Airplane

This exercise is quite simple in terms of directions, but looks much easier than it is in actuality. You stand on one leg, and slowly tilt your body forward. The hips should essentially be the hinge of the turn and both the arms and non-standing leg should be fully extended. Yogis frequently tell people practicing the pose to "act like a Boeing 747." From there, the hips should be opened and extended.

Trap Bar Deadlifts

After loading the trap bar (sometimes called hex bar) with the correct amount of weight, you stand inside the bar and comfortably position yourself with a strong base. Bending your knees, lower your hips to where you can reach the bars. It's important to keep a good posture, with the chest and eyes up. As you raise the bar, it's important to lift up the weight by extending your hips and knees fully. Only once you have reached the maximum do you pull your shoulders back.

Demonstrative Trap Bar Deadlift

2012-2013 Season

Curry's injuries did not worry the Warriors management, as they offered him a four-year contract for $44 million entering the 2012-2013 season. After much rest and rehab, Curry was back in action. On February 27, 2013 he scored 54 points against the New York Knicks. He shot 18 for 28 from the field and went 11 for 13 from behind the arc. The 11 made free throws put Curry just behind Kobe Bryant and Donyell Marshall, for most threes made in any single NBA game. It also had him the title of the **franchise record holder for most 3-pointers scored in a game**. Despite the fact that they lost the game by four points, it was a telling performance for Curry.

Golden State began to do better as well. The Warriors went 47-35, securing a spot in the playoffs as the sixth seed. The Warriors upset the higher seeded Denver Nuggets in six games to advance to the second round. This was Curry's first playoff performance and he handled it quite well. The Warriors advanced to play the San Antonio Spurs, and Curry led off the series scoring 44 points. Despite his efforts, Golden State was knocked out in six games.

Steph Curry playing in his first year in the playoffs

That season Curry also broke the NBA record for the **most amount of 3-pointers made in a single regular season**. Outdoing Ray Allen by three, Steph sunk 272 that year. He also averaged 22.9 points, 4.0 rebounds, 6.9 assists, and 1.6 steals per game during the season.

2013-2014 Season

The Warriors continued to improve the following year, finishing with a 51-31 and again securing the 6th seed heading into the playoffs. Earlier in the season, on December 7th, 2013, Steph broke the Warriors franchise record (previously held by Jason Richardson) for the most three-point field goals made in a career. Steph had already hit 701, in just over four seasons as a professional player.

Despite a stronger record, the Warriors were unable to outlast the Los Angeles Clippers in a 7-game series. Curry put up some impressive performances, including scoring 33 points, 21 of which came from behind the arc, in Game 4 of the series. However, it was not enough to advance the team past the first round.

In addition to scoring 24 points and average 8.5 assists per game, Steph was also named to the **All-NBA Second Team** and made **his first All-Star appearance**. The fans voted him to be a starter in the Western Conference.

Steph Curry playing in his first All-Star Game

2014 -2015 Season

The following year the Warriors were finally able to put it all together, and Curry was showing unprecedented levels of success and growth. The first milestone was hit on January 7, 2015, when **Curry made his 1,000th career 3-point field goal**. He became the fastest player to hit this mark in NBA history. The previous record holder, Dennis Scott, took 457 games to reach the mark. Curry took 369. Less than one month later on February 4, Curry scored 51 points, shooting 16 of 26 from the field, in a win over the Dallas Mavericks. By April 9, 2015, Curry had beaten his 2012-2013 season mark of 272 3-point goals.

In the previous season Lebron James had gotten the most votes for the All-Star Game. However, in 2015, Curry took home the most to overcome James. Having already won the skills challenge, Curry made an attempt to win the 3-point contest.

Steph about to win the 3-Point shooting contest

Just a few months later on May 4, Curry was named the **MVP of the NBA**, the second player (after Wilt Chamberlain) from the Warriors to get the award. During the regular season, Curry ranked first in steals per game, first in free throw percentage, third in 3-point percentage, sixth in points per game, and sixth in assists per game. Essentially, his stats were off the charts.

The Warriors rounded out the season with a 67-15 record, the best in franchise history. They were the first team to win 39 home games in the Western Conference, thus winning 28 games on the road. Additionally, they set records for the longest win streaks of the franchise, with 19 straight at home, 10 while away, and 16 overall.

Thus, the Warriors entered the playoffs with a number 1 seed. The first series was against the New Orleans Pelicans. In Game 1 Curry came off strong, scoring 34 points and leading the Warriors to victory. The Warriors ended up winning the series in 4 games and Steph was proving that he was ready to compete in this postseason. In Game 2 he had 22 points and six assists, in Game 3 he scored 40, and in Game 4 - 39.

In the 6 Game series against the Memphis Grizzlies Steph Curry continued to dominate. In Game 1 the Warriors won by a margin of 15, with Curry putting up 22 and getting 7 assists. In Game 2, despite Curry's 19 points and 6 assists, the Grizzlies were able to take the victory. Again Memphis won game 3, with Curry scoring 23. Golden State rallied back to win games 5 and 6, Curry leading the offensive with 18 points (all from 3-pointers), 7 rebounds, 6 steals, and 5 assists. In Game 6, Curry scored 32 points (24 of which were from beyond the arc and had 10 assists to secure a 13-point victory and advance to the next round.

Curry getting a shot off in the series against the Grizzlies

On paper, the Conference finals were to be very close. Some weren't sure how the Warriors would match up against James Harden, Dwight Howard, and the Houston Rockets. However, Golden State would go on to win in 5 games. Game 1 Steph dropped 34 points en route to a 110-106 victory. Game 2 was much the same, with Curry scoring 33 to overtake the Rockets by 1 point. When the Warriors arrived in Houston for Game 3, Curry game prepared to make a statement, putting up 40 points and 7 assists. The Warriors won 115-80.

In Game 4 Houston came out strong, with James Harden scoring 45 points. Curry had 23 points, but when he took a scary fall, he sat out for 12 minutes to rule out any serious issues or a concussion.

Steph Curry on his way down during scary fall

However, Steph ended up being fine, and came back to score 26, leading the Warriors to a 104-90 win in Game 5, and a trip to the NBA finals against Lebron James' Cleveland Cavaliers.

Also throughout the series Steph gave a new person in his family a chance at the spotlight – his daughter, Riley. She sat on his lap during the press conference, wandered around the stage a little bit and experimented making sounds into the microphone. While some reporters were a bit irked at this, most people found it endearing and it gave Steph a new dimension as a family man.

Steph with his daughter, Riley, at the press conference

The highly anticipated NBA finals got off to an interesting start. Beginning in Oakland, the Warriors took Game 1. Steph curry finished with 26 points and 8 assists to obtain a 108-100 overtime win, despite James' 44 points. The fourth quarter was the James and Curry show, with the two superstars going back and forth, exchanging scores and assists. Unfortunately for the Cavs, key player, Kyrie Irving, left the court in overtime after hurting his knee and was unable to return. Unfortunately, this was the case for the rest of the series.

Cleveland came to Game 2 with a vengeance, and would take the game 95-93, again in overtime. James scored 39 points, had 16 rebounds, and 11 assists. Curry experienced a rare occurrence – a very poor shooting performance. He still scored 19 points, but went an uncharacteristic 5 of 23 from the field. Unfortunately, it wasn't enough to seal a victory.

The first game in Cleveland was rough for the Warriors. Despite a solid effort with Curry scoring 27 points and getting 6 assists, and despite outscoring the Cavs by 12 in the last quarter, Cleveland held off the Warriors with a 96-91 victory. James put up 40 points and had 8 assists, to lead his team to victory.

James and Curry fighting over a loose ball in the finals

The Warriors arrived in Cleveland for Game 4 ready to make a statement. Curry scored 22 points and had 7 assists, and Golden State held James to a meager 21. James also had a rough spill when after banging his head into a camera in the first half, for which he would later need stitches. The Warriors won handedly, 103-82.

The next game in Cleveland was closer, but not close enough. Despite James scoring 40, getting 14 rebounds and 11 assists, the Warriors again won by a significant margin, 104-91. Curry had 37 points, 21 of which were 3-pointers.

Heading back to Cleveland leading the series 3-2 the Warriors had it in mind to win. And they did, handedly. Curry scored 25, had 8 assists, and grabbed 6 rebounds, to end a 40-year championship drought for the Golden State franchise. Curry hit some big shots late in the game to widen the lead and secure a victory. Despite James' 32 points, 18 rebounds, and 9 assists, the Cavs could not hang on. The Warriors won 105-97 in regulation. After the game Curry said:

"I'm kind of speechless. This is special. To be able to hold this trophy and all the hard work we've put into it this season, this is special. We're definitely a great team and a team that should go down in history as one of the best teams from top to bottom."

Steph Curry and Andre Iguodala sharing the sweetness of victory

The leader of this Warrior team gets commended for more than just his skills and style of play. *His character, and his humility, are what many said makes the real Steph Curry.*

Shaun Livingston, for example, told USA Today that *"He's one of the most humble superstars there is, by far. His Faith, his beliefs, and his value system is unprecedented. [On the court] it's his style of play, for one. He's a showman, but at the same time he doesn't show people up. That's hard to do in this league, because there's a line that you can cross by playing that way. His humility kind of resonates throughout the locker room."*

What is impressive about Curry, and what puts him in the same category as other greats, is **his dedication to the sport**. The Coach of the Nike Skills Academy, who first worked with Kobe Bryant, has explain Steph's continuous work ethic as an above and beyond approach. Steph, who too attended the Skills Academy, the coach now says was *"the least recognized player there."*

At the Skills Academy the athletes had two workouts every day for three days. The coaches noticed that Curry was always prepared way before the other players. Thirty minutes before every workout, when many athletes were still arriving at the gym, and beginning to get dressed, Curry was already laced up and ready to go, often practicing form shooting before the players began playing. Often before the drills even started, he would have made over 100 shots. After the workout, before leaving the court, he would ensure to swish five free-throws in a row, on tired legs and with tired arms.

Even with the level of success he has achieved, and the level that he is at, Curry maintains this work ethic. **He is still the first player to get to the gym, and the last one to leave.** He works constantly and tirelessly, and even after winning distinguished awards, he constantly finds things to work and improve upon.

CHAPTER 4

FAMILY & FAITH

"There's more to me than just this jersey I wear, and that's Christ living inside of me"
– Stephen Curry

Despite his fame and glory, Curry maintains a strong sense of normalcy, with a strong emphasis placed on family. Aside from bringing his daughter on stage with him to the press conference, and let her roam around and make sounds into the microphone, he and his wife, Ayesha Curry, have posted things on social media of their normal routine, including goofing around.

One such example is a video the couple made called *"Chef Curry With the Pot"* – spoof of Drake's "0 to 100." In the video the couple dances, and Ayesha lip syncs about cooking. It's quite amusing and garnered over 3 million views in a quick period of time.

Having grown up in a family with a father as a professional athlete, Curry attributes his effortless abilities to his father, who easily managed his basketball life and family life. Stephs's wife, Ayesha, has a blog (littlelightsofmine.com) dedicated to faith, food, and family. Steph often participates in social media efforts for the website, acting as a video guest.

Curry's mother started a Christian Montessori School when he was growing up, and religion has played a significant role in his life. He was raised going to Church every Sunday for services, and he also attended Bible studies every Wednesday.

Steph has explained that he was in fourth grade when he began to hear and understand the gospel of Jesus Christ, as he walked down the Church aisle to give his life to him. At Charlotte Christian High School the students prayed daily. Curry frequently attributes his adversities and the steps that he's taken in his life to a higher power. He even mentioned the decision to play for Bob McKillop at Davidson was made more comfortable because of the fact that McKillop was a man of faith.

On his arm, Steph has the Hebrew version of Corinthians 13:8, tattooed. It reads: "*Love never fails. But where there are prophecies, they will cease; where there are tongues, they will be stilled; where there is knowledge, it will pass away.*"

Finally, Curry has released videos and spoken openly about his faith and how it has affected his career. He claims that it keeps him grounded, focused, balanced, and has enabled him to end up in the right scenarios.

CHAPTER 5

EXCLUSIVE DRILLS
AND EXERCISES
USED BY
STEPHEN CURRY

"I want to practice to the point where it's almost uncomfortable how fast you shoot, so that in the game things kind of slow down"
– Stephen Curry

Steph has done some remarkable things now, and is likely to continue improving. His success story – the small scrawny kid who faced and overcame injuries is a compelling one – and people are certainly attracted to his work ethic. But, **what exactly was Steph Curry doing during these times to improve his game gradually, and get to the level where he is at today?** What kinds of drills was he conducting on a daily basis, that have led to him scoring well into the double-digits, handling the ball better than anyone on the court, and delivering passes that few people can comprehend.

Shooting Drills

Curry has a range of skills, but what makes him a candidate to be a potential legend is definitely his shot. At the age of 27, people are already debating if he is the best shooter the sport has ever seen. This certainly dates back to the summer in high school, when he and his father worked to change his form to release the ball over his head, and get his shot off miraculously quickly.

A *Wall Street Journal* article broke down **the science behind Curry's unbe-**

lievable shot. For example, aside from his overhead release point, he takes only 0.3 seconds to release the ball, which is about 0.1 seconds faster than many of the other top shooters in the NBA – a significant percentage margin when put into perspective. Additionally, he has a higher arc than the average shooter. His 3-point attempts hit a peak height of 16.23 feet, whereas the maximum average of other shooters is closer to 15.77. The extra height, according to experts, allows the ball to enter the hoop at a more favorable angle – at least 45 degrees.

It should be noted **the quantity of shots that Curry takes**. During the off-season, he says he makes about 500 shots a day. Not takes, makes. And during the season, it's a bit lower, anywhere between 200 and 350 depending on the schedule. What he maintains though, is that whatever goal is set, he will never cut it short. *"If I play Around the World, I have to make 10 out of 13 at each of the seven sports to move on,"* he says. *"If I don't, I'll sit at that same spot until I do."*

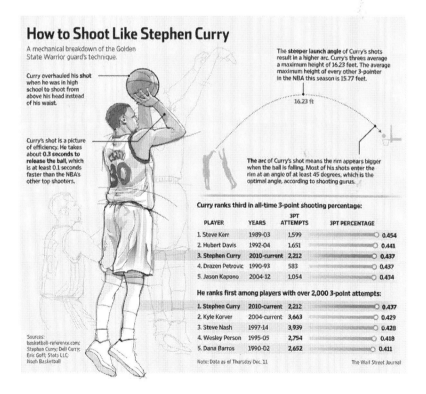

How to Shoot Like Stephen Curry

A mechanical breakdown of the Golden State Warrior guard's technique.

Curry overhauled his shot when he was in high school to shoot from above his head instead of his waist.

Curry's shot is a picture of efficiency. He takes about 0.3 seconds to release the ball, which is at least 0.1 seconds faster than the NBA's other top shooters.

The steeper launch angle of Curry's shots result in a higher arc. Curry's threes average a maximum height of 16.23 feet. The average maximum height of every other 3-pointer in the NBA this season is 15.77 feet.

16.23 ft

The arc of Curry's shot means the rim appears bigger when the ball is falling. Most of his shots enter the rim at an angle of at least 45 degrees, which is the optimal angle, according to shooting gurus.

Curry ranks third in all-time 3-point shooting percentage:

PLAYER	YEARS	3PT ATTEMPTS	3PT PERCENTAGE	
1. Steve Kerr	1989-03	1,599		0.454
2. Hubert Davis	1992-04	1,651		0.441
3. Stephen Curry	2010-current	2,212		0.437
4. Drazen Petrovic	1990-93	583		0.437
5. Jason Kapono	2004-12	1,054		0.434

He ranks first among players with over 2,000 3-point attempts:

PLAYER	YEARS	3PT ATTEMPTS	3PT PERCENTAGE	
1. Stephen Curry	2010-current	2,212		0.437
2. Kyle Korver	2004-current	3,663		0.429
3. Steve Nash	1997-14	3,939		0.428
4. Wesley Person	1995-05	2,754		0.418
5. Dana Barros	1990-02	2,652		0.411

Sources: basketball-reference.com; Stephen Curry; Dell Curry; Eric Goff; Stats LLC; Noah Basketball

Note: Data as of Thursday Dec. 11

The Wall Street Journal

Form Shooting Drill

One of many of Steph's warm-up drills is a simple form shooting drill. Simultaneously while dribbling with his left hand, he takes one handed right hand shots from just a few feet from the basket. This not only allows him to practice his dribbling form while looking away from the ball and being focused on two activities, but also reinforces his learned shooting form. Steph will often then expand on the basics of this drill, moving to different points of the court. He'll then even do one-step shots as he shoots.

Elbow-In Drill

Another aspect of Steph Curry's shooting form that many gurus note is how he tucks in his elbow. In order to practice this, Steph will often do a drill where he crosses over between cones and well come to the elbow where he pivots in, squares his elbow up perpendicular to the rim, and releases a shot.

Shooting Conditioning Drill

This is a drill that Steph does on a regular basis, both in practice and before games. He'll start on one side at the wing and take an outside shot (usually a 3). From there, he'll run to half court. As he is making the spring a rebounder passes to a passer at the top of the key. If he made the shot, he'll get a pass again from beyond the arc on the same side wing from the passer, and take another shot. However, if he missed the initial shot, he'll come to jump stop as he catches the ball. Make a move and take a dribble, and take a closer-range shot.

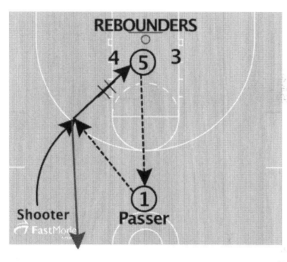

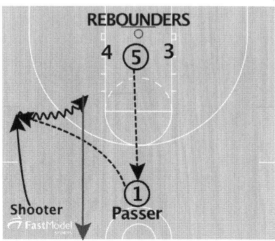

Once Bounce Drill

Standing at the bottom of the court Steph will pass the ball to a coach at the top of the key. The coach will then toss the ball anywhere on the court, and Steph has to sprint and catch the ball without letting up more than one bounce. Further, he'll need to jump and come to a full jump stop, standing in triple threat, with squared feet, and then take a quick shot. The drill can also be done with other players at the bottom of the key, and the coach selecting whose turn it is.

Dribbling Drills

When Steph realized his potential in the professional basketball world would be in the point guard position, he began aggressively increasing his dribbling skills. His ball handling skills have improved tenfold over the years, and he still does a range of activities to keep these skills honed. While he still does a number of two-ball dribbling drills, he has expanded his repertoire to including other unrelated stimuli, to his routine. These are some examples of the drills that he does in addition to many of the two ball sets, on a regular basis.

Tennis Ball Dribbling Drill

To focus on dribbling, looking up, being aware, and excessive stimuli, Curry frequently does a comprehensive dribbling drill. This includes dribbling quickly while a partner stands behind him (in his case a drills coach). The coach stands behind him, where his is dribbling stationary, and throws a tennis ball at a wall about five feet in front of him. Curry catches the ball on either side it is thrown. If he has the ball in his left hand, and the tennis ball is coming to his right side, he has to quickly cross over to catch the ball. He then throws the ball back against the wall to his coach, and the drill continues.

Behind-The-Back Pass Dribbling

This drill involves two extra partners. As Steph stands dribbling with one hand, a person stands in front of him and bounces him a ball to his left hand. Steph takes one simultaneous dribble with his left hand and then whips the ball behind his back to another participant on his side. The participant throws the ball to the first feeder and the drill continues.

Wrist-Weight Dribbling

In order to work on the speed and strength of his dribbling, Steph will often put weights on his wrists while he does a series of dribbling. He'll do some basic drills like one-handed cross overs and back and forth pullbacks. Adding the weight to the drill makes removing the weight feel as though his hands are lighter. It also further strengthens the muscles used while dribbling, so when it is late in the game, he feels less fatigued.

Triple Crossover

Although a fairly basic drill, Steph will still practice Triple Crossovers with intent on a regular basis. This drill is exactly what it sounds like – three consecutive crossovers from one hand to the other, with a dribble in one outside hand in between. The key is to be forceful, have good form, and always be looking up.

Fan, Crossover, Between the Legs, Behind the Back

Another Curry staple drill is the fan, crossover, between the legs, behind the back. Essentially you just follow the steps above, with only a break dribble in the middle. After a one handed fan or cross over, you cross the ball over to the other hand, from where it goes straight back to the opposite side between the legs. Once the ball is the in the opposite hand behind your back, you throw it behind the back to the other side, before bringing back around to repeat.

Stephen Curry Skills Academy

Ryan Goodson, who is the director of the *Stephen Curry Skills Academy*, demonstrates the drills below. Goodson and Curry worked together in 2011 at a Skills Academy and he learned of the old two-ball dribbling drills that made him the point guard he is today.

In order to do so, he spent a lot of time practicing dribbling drills. Namely, two-ball dribbling drills. Today, Steph can be seen doing some of these drills during his pregame warm up. Today the Stephen Curry Skills Academy highlights many of the drills that were transformative for Steph at the time. They should be done for 30 seconds each and they include:

Two-Ball Same

This one is pretty self-explanatory. You take two balls and simultaneously and forcefully dribble them into the ground while knees are bent and back is relatively straight.

Two-Ball Alternate

Standing still, knees bent, back straight, this is a dribbling drill where you have a ball in both hands and dribble. As the ball in one hand hits the floor, the ball in the other hand should be up in the palm.

Two-Ball between the Legs

For the two ball between the legs drill, you dribble simultaneously. When you dribble one ball between the legs, you crossover the other ball into the other hand. The pattern continues.

Two-Ball Cross-Over

Followed by two simultaneous dribbles with each hand, you take the two balls and cross them over. Make it a point to always but the right hand ball in front of the left, or vice versa. Alternatively, you can switch which ball is in front to increase the level of difficulty.

Two-Ball behind the Back

Like the crossover this drill starts with two simultaneous dribbles and then you take one hand and throw the ball behind the back. As you throw one ball behind the back you cross the other ball over to the other hand.

Two-Ball under Dribble

As in the previous drills, begin with two simultaneous dribbles. Then take one ball and dribble through your legs from behind. With the other ball cross it over to the opposite hand simultaneously.

Two-Ball between the Legs Cross Over

In order to do this drill you must isolate one leg, or rather, one side to use. After two simultaneous dribbles you take one ball and cross it through your legs, from the front, to the other side of the body. At the same time, cross the other ball in front of you to the opposite hand, and whip that hand back to retrieve the ball through your legs.

Two-Ball between the Legs behind the Back

Admittedly, this drill looks very complicated. It should be done once you have successfully reached the point where you can do the two-ball dribbling behind the back and between the legs. After two simultaneous dribbles, you take one hand and dribble one ball through your legs from the front to the back. With the other hand you cross over the ball in front. As you retrieve the ball in the back, instead of bring it around to the front, you cross it over to the other side of your body behind you with a behind the back dribble. At the same time as this behind the back dribble, you cross over the ball in front back to the original side.

8. Between the Legs-Behind the Back

Two-Ball inside Leg

After two simultaneous dribbles you will again cross one ball through the legs. However, unlike the previous drills, the ball is crossed through the legs from the front, and to the same-hand side. Thus, the balls stay in the same hand throughout the drill. After doing one of the right side, the right will stay stationary as you do two simultaneous dribbles, and then to the inside through the legs dribble with your left hand.

9. Inside Leg

3 Ball Commando

Once you have all the previous drills down, you can really challenge yourself with the 3 Ball Commando. Essentially, this is a test, or a combination, of all the drills preceding it. You take a third ball and throw it up in the air, letting it bounce. For a few seconds as the loose ball bounces, you commence with one of the two-ball drills. After you finish the few seconds, you bounce one of the balls down hard, let it bounce, and move on to the next drill with the two balls. The objective is to move on throughout the drills while keeping all the balls alive and preventing any of them from ceasing to bounce. It's quite difficult but a great ultimate test after you've finished the drill set.

In fact, you can see Stephen Curry still doing a number of these dribbling drills before a game today:

Rebounding Drills

As a point guard, Steph is not expected to grab a high number of rebounds, but he does occasionally get near the double digits. Adding this dimension to his game has made him an even more dynamic player than he already was – an impressive feat.

Resistance Band Rebounding

In order to emulate and make the motion of rebounding more difficult, Steph will be tied down with resistance bands that are attached to the ground. However, if you don't have resistance bands, getting some sort of weight vest, or adding weight in any extra way, will work well. Then, with a ball or medicine ball in his hands, he'll jump up as if to grab for a rebound. His coaches, trainers, teammates, etc., stand beside him hitting him with pads to emulate the contact that happens in a game.

Strength Training

Steph Curry is listed at 6'3" and 185 pounds. While still small, Curry's stature has noticeably changed even since his Davidson days. Size has been a common apprehension among coaches and scouts in the past, and subsequently, something that Curry has made a central point of his training. While he is still by no means a large player in the NBA, he consistently works on his strength so that he is not at all hindered by this disadvantage. Here are some consistent strength routines that Steph practices.

Explosiveness Drill

Another thing Steph does early in a typical practice day is a drill that focuses on explosiveness. His trainer holds a resistance band, which is strapped around Steph's waist, firmly. From there, Steph takes explosive drives to either side with the resistance. This makes him quicker on his feet without the band, and ideally more explosive on both his left and right side.

Ladder-Core Exercise

After setting up two floor ladders Steph will run quickly with one foot in each to the end. Once finished, he'll jump up high and go right into a make-shift burpee. For the burpee he jumps down into a wide push up position, with his feet separated as well, and hops right back up to go back on the opposite ladder.

Rope Drills

Using two heavy ropes, Steph will do a series of exercises that help to increase his upper body strength. He'll begin aggressively and dramatically throwing the ropes up while alternating the arms up and down. Then he'll progress into a simultaneous up and down motion. Afterwards, he'll effectively do jumping jacks while throwing the ropes up in the air. After a few seconds rest, he brings in a ball to make the drill more basketball-specific. As he dribbles with one hand, on the other side he aggressively throws the rope up and down in sync with his tempo. Then he will switch hands and the set is complete. The entire set lasts about a minute but is done with the upmost intensity.

Lunge Series

To emulate and dramatize some of the jab steps, step backs, and lunges that players naturally make in a game, Steph incorporates weights in a lunge series. He takes two heavy dumbbells, one in each hand and does a range of motions with them. This includes an exaggerated lunge to one side, stepping back and bringing the dumbbells over his head, and stretching his mobile leg all the way to the other side. Then he will switch legs and do an exaggerated lunge to one side, while holding the weights.

Game Simulations

As most NBA players do, and as all good basketball players should, Steph does a range of game simulation drills. Practicing repetition of a variety of situations, and subsequent ways to handle the situations, is a good way to develop instincts and reactionary tactics.

Separation 1 on 1 Drill

One drill Steph does with teammates is a 1 on 1 drill with a limited amount of space. He sets up two cones, about ten feet apart between above the three-point line. With only three dribbles, he is supposed to stay between the cones, and fine a way to score.

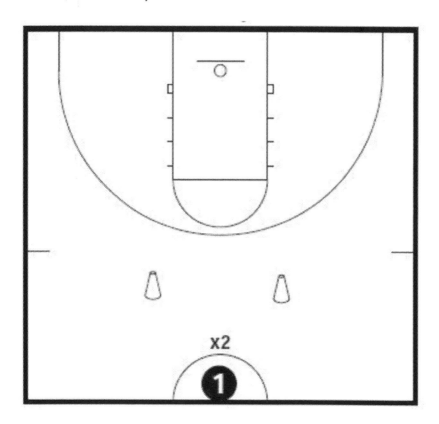

Dribble Attack 1-on-1

This drill is for both offense and defense. Two players start out on opposite sides of the same baseline. There are two chairs set up on the respective 3-point wings. When someone blows the whistle or indicates a start, both players must run up and around the outside of the chair to the inside of the court. The offensive player, of course, must dribble, giving the defender a chance to get a step ahead. Once the players are around the chair it is a game of 1-on-1. This simulates the fast paced 1-on-1 situations that happen in games, often on fast breaks.

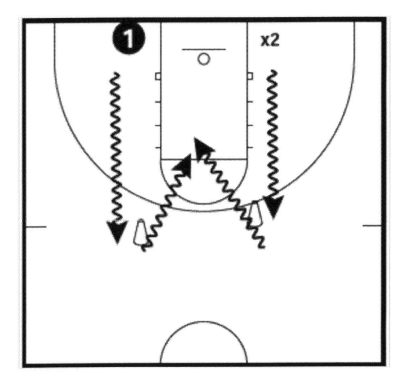

Jab Series 1-on-1

In this scenario, an offensive player and defensive player are positioned together below the rim. The offensive player has to find a way to get open on one of the wings. They only have five seconds to get open otherwise the round is over. A person at the top of the key will deliver a pass to the person once they are open. After the player gets open it is 1-on-1 with a small caveat: there is a limit of 3 dribbles and only one shot. If the offense scores they play offense again.

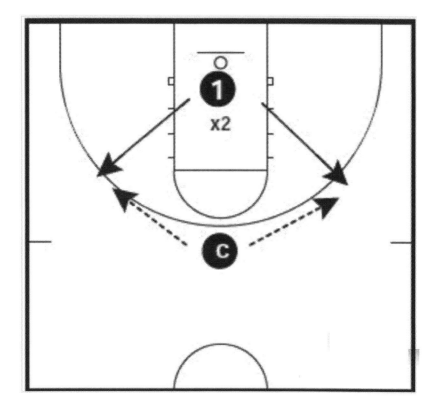

Pre-Game Warm-Up

Coaches often say that how you warm up dictates how you will play. It's important to emphasize the warm up, as you are quite literally conditioning and preparing yourself for the game ahead. Thus, taking the warm-up seriously is critical.

Often on game days the Warriors have a shoot around for about an hour in the morning. The session is informal and relaxed, but is used just to begin to get in the mindset. Following the shoot-around and some rest, they arrive at the arena a few hours before the game. About an hour and half before game time Steph does a comprehensive warm-up to sharpen up, get focused and prepared.

Two-Ball Dribbling

Curry begins his pre-game warm-up at the arena with a series of two-ball dribbling drills. This includes simultaneous dribbling with both hands, alternating dribbling, going behind the back, and between the legs. He begins this way to stay focused and get a feel for the ball before the game. These are many of the drills that he began practicing in high school and college to become a better point guard.

After some two-ball dribbling he'll switch to one ball drills. A teammate will roll or pass him a ball and he will dribble, always very hard and with intention, doing crossovers, between the legs, etc.

One-Step Shots

From here he will go to various places on the court and take one-step shots. He begins with some scoop shots from close to the hoop. This is to warm up and begin to get confident, watching the ball continuously going in the net. Then he'll move back and take some one step shots from farther out.

3-Point Shots

Finally, he'll move beyond the arc. He'll take a number of 3-pointers now. He says he usually takes around 105-110, and likes to make about 70 or above. He'll do a range of moves for the shot. He'll dribble to his left or his right then step back and take a shot. He may step inside and hop back out before shooting. He'll sprint to the corner, catch and shoot. Then he'll spring to the top of the key and shoot. Then he'll dribble quickly for a quick shot. He essentially emulates the range of shots that he'll take in a game.

1-on-1 session

With his trainer, he'll do a series of 1-on-1 scenarios as his coach leans on him and pushes him. Then Steph will take some fade away shots, pull up shots, and others that are often taken in one go.

After the session he is still about an hour away from game time. He'll head back into the locker room for any necessary treatment and to prepare both mentally and physical for the upcoming game.

CHAPTER 6

5 INTERESTING FACTS YOU DIDN'T KNOW ABOUT STEPH CURRY

1. When Curry arrives at the Oracle Arena for games he has three superstitions: he always backs into his spot and then waves to the female parking attendant in the parking lot, and then proceeds to hug various security officers.
2. According to The Count's video review of his 337 free throws this season, Curry shot 89.5% with his mouth guard visible in his mouth, but he shot 92.5% when the mouth guard was out of his mouth.
3. When Steph was 8 years old he played in an exhibition during halftime of the 1996 Nike Hoop Summit high school all-star game in Charlotte.
4. Charlotte Christian School celebrates Stephen Curry Day on May 8.
5. He has his own line of Under Armour shoes. They have a small number "30" along the edge.

CHAPTER 7

TOP 5 MOTIVATIONAL LESSONS FROM STEPHEN CURRY

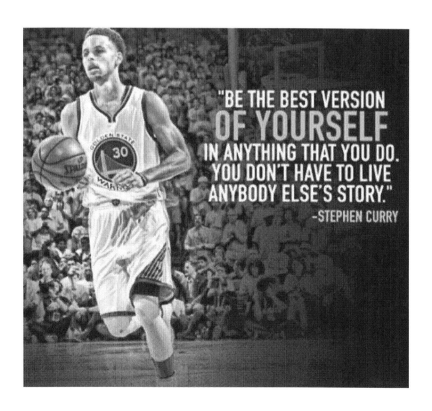

"BE THE BEST VERSION OF YOURSELF IN ANYTHING THAT YOU DO. YOU DON'T HAVE TO LIVE ANYBODY ELSE'S STORY."

-STEPHEN CURRY

1. Early is on time

All of Steph's coaches have mentioned throughout the years that Steph was often the first one to practice at the gym, and was intensely apologetic if something came up. Generally speaking, if Curry wasn't at least 30 minutes early, he considered himself late.

2. Never Give Up, Don't Listen to Doubters

Despite the support of his family and many other friends, throughout Steph's upbringing many people doubted his potential. Frequently, this was due to his size. They admired his big dreams, but thought that Steph was simply too small to be able to play. That said, he never let that stop him from working hard to try and achieve his goals. Ultimately, that perseverance has helped him get to where he is today.

3. Get/Find a Supportive Network

In line with the previous point, Steph was certain to establish a strong support system throughout the years. Of course the most noted example was his father, who helped Steph train and alter his shot from a young age. His brother, too, not only provided a support system, but also a training partner throughout their childhoods. Additionally, his mother, and now his wife and child, all give him extra support. For an athlete, their life off the court can often influence their life on the court. Thus, establishing and maintaining a strong support network is critically important.

4. Repeat, Repeat, Repeat

One thing that all of Steph's coaches have reiterated – from high school, to college, to the NBA – is that Steph is a disciplined athlete. He does drills time and time again, until he not only gets it perfectly, but gets it perfectly numerous times.

5. Never Be Satisfied; Always Look to Improve

Despite his getting better every season, Steph is never satisfied. He finished as the MVP scoring well into the double-digits every game, but is constantly looking to improve on new aspects of his game. He'll constantly make the point that until he is shooting 100%, there is always something to work on.

CHAPTER 8

AWARDS AND RECOGNITION

2016

- Best Record Breaking Performance ESPY Award
- NBA MVP
- All-NBA First Team
- NBA Scoring Leader
- NBA Steals Leader

2015

- NBA MVP
- Best Male Athlete ESPY Award
- Best NBA Player ESPY Award
- All-NBA Team
- NBA Player of the Week
- Three Point Shootout Champion
- Western All-Star Fan Vote Selection

2014

- All-NBA Second Team
- NBA Player of the Month
- NBA Player of the Week
- Three Point Shootout Participant
- Western All-Star Fan Vote Selection

2013

- NBA Player of the Month
- Three Point Shootout Participant

2011

- NBA Sportsmanship Award
- All-Star Skills Challenge Champion
- Rising Stars Challenge Participant

2010

- NBA Rookie of the Month (3 months)
- Rising Stars Challenge Participant
- Three Point Shootout Participant

2009

- Consensus All-American First Team

- NABC All-American First Team
- AP All-American First Team
- USBWA All-American First Team
- Sporting News All-American Second team
- SoCon Player of the Year
- Southern Conference Tournament MOP
- SoCon First Team All-Tournament

2008

- Consensus All-American Second
- AP All-American Second Team
- SoCon Player of the Year
- Southern Conference Tournament MOP
- SoCon First Team All-Tournament

2007

- Southern Conference Tournament MOP
- SoCon First Team All-Tournament
- SoCon Freshman of the Year
- SoCon All-Freshman Team

CHAPTER 9

NBA SEASON STATS

Season	Games Played	Points	Assists	Rebounds	Steals	Average Minutes	Field Goal pct.
2015-2016	79	30.1	6.7	5.4	2.1	34.2	.504
2014-2015	80	23.8	7.7	4.3	2.0	32.7	.487
2013-2014	78	24.0	8.5	4.3	1.6	36.5	.471
2012-2013	78	22.9	6.9	4.0	1.6	38.2	.451
2011-2012	26	14.7	5.3	3.4	1.5	28.2	.490
2010-2011	74	18.6	5.8	3.9	1.5	33.6	.480
2009-2010	80	17.5	5.9	4.5	1.9	36.2	.462

CONCLUSION

Steph Curry has had an interesting trajectory that has led him to where he is today – one of the most respected basketball players and possibly one of the best shooters of all time. Many would have expected that a kid who grew up into a stable financial family, and with a father who was a professional in the sport, would have had a fairly smooth and easy ride to success. However, Steph did not seamlessly rise to the top, as people could never move past his size – or rather, lack thereof.

All that said, though Steph's story is one that is impressive, and should be recognized for its unusualness, is not necessarily a mystery. Any coach that has worked with him throughout his life has commended Steph's rigorous work ethic, and unwillingness to give up. He is always the first to arrive at the gym, and the last to leave practice.

Steph is a player that believes in utter commitment. He always sought to execute every drill to the best of his ability. Not only would he show up and continuously repeat drills and strategies that make him the player he is now, but he would do so with an unmistakable effort.

Further, he truly believes in the spirit of a team. Even when his stats are off the charts, Steph knows that he needs the people around him in order to succeed. Despite his statistics and stardom, this is something that separates this player from many others.

The drills that have led Steph to success will not yield results in and of themselves. It's that he fully committed himself to them, bought into the practices, and delivered each repetition with intent. While he has had endless support from his father, family, and coaches along the way, his ability to fully commit and devote himself to bettering every aspect of his game has led him to the success he has had, and will likely continue to have for years to come. And that is something that cannot always be taught.

ABOUT THE AUTHOR

Steve James isn't your typical sports fan. While there are some that will always make time to watch the big game, James started following the NBA at a very young age and has watched some of the best players in the history of the NBA from the very beginning. Even at that young age, he started paying attention to who was really standing out on the court–greats like Michael Jordan, Magic Johnson or Larry Bird. Steve follows the game till this date and knows the ins and outs of the greatest NBA stars of today, like Kobe Bryant, LeBron James, Kevin Durant or Stephen Curry. Having carefully watched these players on the court and studied their lives, he has a unique perspective into their success, how it was achieved, and what makes them so great.

He has an insider view into the secrets that have made these players so successful. By collecting this information into his books, he hopes to help not just young, aspiring basketball players, but all people to learn the secrets of what it takes to be successful. By looking at how these players have reached their goals, the readers will glean the information they need to reach their own goals. Steve's years of analyzing play styles, successes, failures, training routines, etc. gives him a real insight into these players!

Printed in Great Britain
by Amazon

32582042R00047